SUPER™ **QAR**

for Test-Wise Students

Student Activity Book

This book belongs to:

D1472103

Wright Group

A Trunkful of Treasures

Amanda watched as Gram reached into the trunk and gently lifted out a red and green quilt. "You see, these quilts have been passed down through each generation of our family. Each one carries the spirit of the people who made it. Their stories are waiting for someone like you."

Suddenly a moth fluttered out of the trunk.

"Oh, dear," Gram said, shaking her head. "The moths have eaten holes in them!"

Amanda saw the disappointment on Gram's face. "Are they ruined?" Amanda asked.

Gram sighed. "No, but they'll need a little mending, and my eyes aren't as sharp as they used to be."

"I can help you," Amanda volunteered. "I'm good with a needle and thread."

Gram's smile returned. "Let's carry them down to the living room by the fireplace and get working."

Minutes later, Amanda was sitting with Gram on the old green couch surrounded by a rainbow of colorful quilts in every pattern and size.

"Which one should we mend first?" Amanda asked.

"Let's start with the oldest one," Gram said, pointing to a quilt dominated by big bold blocks. Each block was framed in red.

"Do you know who made this quilt, Gram?"

"I certainly do…"

QUESTION AND ANSWER	**QAR**

1. Have you ever used a needle and thread?

    _____
    _____

2. What fluttered out of the trunk when Gram lifted out the first quilt?

    _____
    _____
    _____

3. What could Amanda do to help Gram since her eyesight wasn't good?

    _____
    _____
    _____

4. Why did Gram look disappointed when she saw the moths had eaten holes in the quilts? _____

    _____
    _____

5. What is Gram going to tell Amanda next?

    _____
    _____
    _____

1. _____
   _____

2. _____
   _____

3. _____
   _____

4. _____
   _____

5. _____
   _____

The Bear's Paw

"My great-great-great-grandfather, George Fry, was born more than 150 years ago in a country called Wales. In 1824, he and his family made a long sea voyage across the Atlantic Ocean to come to the United States. He was only two years old when his family traveled to settle in the Michigan Territory.

"When he was eight years old, the family built a log cabin in the woods.

"George was a brave and adventurous lad. But he was afraid of one thing: bears! He and his sister made this quilt after a close encounter with a 'grizzly.'"

George Fry

George Fry's my name, and the scariest thing that ever happened to me was in the spring of 1830. I remember one day Mama took the wagon into town to buy supplies. She told me and my twelve-year-old sister Louisa to take care of the house and look after baby Ina.

For the past month a bear, hungry after hibernating, had been pestering the horses and cattle.

"Don't worry, George," sixteen-year-old Herschal told me. "I won't let that ol' grizzly get you. Me and Pa are going out this afternoon to find it."

Pa and Herschal hadn't been gone an hour when all of a sudden Louisa and I heard a loud crash outside on the woodpile, a scratching sound like claws up the wall, then a thundering and a banging right up over our heads.

Directions: Think of some questions that could be answered from reading the text on page 4. Write at least one question under each QAR heading. After each question write the answer in parenthesis.

In the Book—Right There

_____

_____

_____

_____

_____

_____

_____

In My Head—On My Own

_____

_____

_____

_____

_____

_____

_____

In the Book—Think and Search

_____

_____

_____

_____

_____

_____

_____

In My Head—Author and Me

_____

_____

_____

_____

_____

_____

_____

Shuttling Through Space

The space shuttle crews have fun, but they work hard, too. They perform all kinds of scientific experiments. They also launch, fix, and capture satellites and other equipment.

Many famous firsts have taken place on space shuttle missions. Guion (Guy) Bluford was the first African American astronaut. Bluford's first shuttle flight was on the *Challenger* in 1983. He traveled to space four times.

Sally Ride became the first American woman in space, also in 1983. She flew two missions and then went to work at NASA headquarters in Washington, D.C.

By 1999, the space program had many female astronauts, but not one female pilot. Eileen Collins became the first woman to land a spacecraft of any kind.

NASA also planned to use the shuttle to launch the first teacher into space. Christa McAuliffe was chosen to join the *Challenger* crew in 1986. Her job was to teach lessons about space that would be shared with classrooms all over the country.

But on January 28, 1986, as millions of students watched on TV, the *Challenger* exploded two minutes after liftoff. All the astronauts were killed. Americans were stunned, especially by McAuliffe's tragic death.

The *Challenger* tragedy reminded Americans once again of the great risks of space travel. After the accident, all space flights were cancelled while the shuttle was redesigned.

1. What famous firsts have taken place on shuttle missions? _____

   1. _____

   _____

   _____

2. Until the 1980s there were no women and African Americans in the space program. Can you think of reasons why?

   2. _____

   _____

   _____

   _____

3. Who was the first African American astronaut? _____

   3. _____

   _____

   _____

4. How do you think Eileen Collins felt about being the first female pilot in the space program? _____

   4. _____

   _____

   _____

5. What are some of the jobs astronauts do in space? _____

   5. _____

   _____

   _____

Building a Rocket

Gravity is the force that holds us on Earth and keeps us from flying into space. A rocket powerful enough to break through Earth's gravity would have to carry tons of fuel. But a rocket big enough to carry so much fuel would be too heavy to fly very fast. Space flight seemed impossible.

Instead of building rockets in one big piece, scientists realized they could build rockets in sections, called stages. The bottom stages would carry fuel. The top stage would carry the payload, or cargo. It would be the only part of the rocket that would orbit in space.

Stages allowed rockets to fly higher than ever before. When the first stage has used all its fuel, it falls off. But the rocket continues to rise because the fuel in the next stage begins to burn right away. After each stage drops off, the rocket flies even faster and farther because it becomes lighter. The process goes on until the payload reaches space and enters an orbit around the earth.

QUESTION

ANSWER	QAR	STRATEGY USED

Hot Work

Imagine gazing down a hole that reaches deep inside the earth. With every breath you take, you're nearly overcome by a stink worse than the smell of rotten eggs.

Imagine crawling past a river of lava. As the lava rushes by, it hisses and bubbles and you fear that the ground beneath you might crumble at any minute.

These images may seem like scenes from an exciting movie. But for volcanologists Maurice and Katia Krafft, moments like these were all in a day's work.

Volcanologists are scientists that study the many different aspects of volcanoes. Some volcanologists might never visit a volcano. Instead, they work in a laboratory and study volcanic rocks. By looking at these rocks, volcanologists can learn how a volcano acted while it erupted. Other volcanologists may study only dormant, or inactive, volcanoes. Dormant volcanoes can help scientists understand past eruptions and the earth's history.

The study of active volcanoes is the most direct—and dangerous— way to learn about volcanoes. By watching volcanoes as they erupt, volcanologists can learn why volcanoes erupt and how to predict future eruptions. Volcanologists Maurice and Katia Krafft loved the thrill and adventure of standing beside an erupting volcano. They dedicated their lives to the study of active volcanoes around the world.

Directions: Read each question and its four answer choices. Select the best answer for each question. Then identify the QAR and tell why you think this is the best answer.

1. What do volcanoes smell worse than?

   A. wood smoke

   B. rotten eggs

   C. bubbling water

   D. hissing rivers

   QAR: _____

   Why is this the best answer?

   _____

   _____

   _____

2. How did Maurice and Katia Krafft feel about their jobs?

   A. scared and nervous

   B. like they were in a movie

   C. they loved the thrill and adventure

   D. none of the above

   QAR: _____

   Why is this the best answer?

   _____

   _____

   _____

3. Which of these is a place to study volcanoes?

   A. in a laboratory

   B. at dormant volcanoes

   C. at active volcanoes

   D. all of the above

   QAR: _____

   Why is this the best answer?

   _____

   _____

   _____

4. Which of these cannot be learned from studying volcanoes?

   A. how a volcano acted while it erupted

   B. why volcanoes erupt

   C. how to predict future eruptions

   D. how rocks are formed

   QAR: _____

   Why is this the best answer?

   _____

   _____

   _____

Always an Adventure

Maurice and Katia had many adventures while studying volcanoes. They traveled to the Great Rift in Africa to study a bubbling pool of lava. There they hiked deep into a volcano's crater. They set up camp in the crater, where they worked for fifteen days. Katia said it was like being inside "the bowels of the earth."

One of their wildest adventures was on a volcanic lake in Indonesia known as "The Green Crater." This lake, made of acid, was formed after a volcano erupted. Acid is a liquid that can eat away at many things, including skin! If Maurice and Katia had fallen in the acid lake, their bodies would have dissolved within an hour. They floated out on the lake in an acid-proof rubber boat. Then they carefully took samples of the acid with a bottle attached to the end of a metal cable. When the acid ate through the metal cable, they had to stop taking samples.

1. What is being inside a crater like?

Answer: _____

_____

QAR: _____

Possible multiple-choice answers:

A. _____

_____

_____

_____

B. _____

_____

_____

C. _____

_____

_____

D. _____

_____

_____

2. Why was working in "The Green Crater" dangerous for Maurice and Katia?

Answer: _____

_____

QAR: _____

Possible multiple-choice answers:

A. _____

_____

_____

B. _____

_____

_____

C. _____

_____

_____

D. _____

_____

_____

3. How do you suppose Maurice and Katia felt when they camped inside a volcano's crater?

Answer: _____

_____

QAR: _____

Possible multiple-choice answers:

A. _____

_____

_____

B. _____

_____

_____

C. _____

_____

_____

D. _____

_____

_____

Directions: Brainstorm as many criteria as you can for the following questions. Remember to think about open-ended answers as well as multiple-choice. Write down all your ideas on this page.

What makes a good response to a Think and Search question?

_____

_____

_____

_____

_____

_____

_____

What makes a good response to an Author and Me question?

_____

_____

_____

_____

_____

_____

_____

_____

A Strange Foreign Girl

When my alarm rings the next morning, I roll over and pull the covers over my head. I wonder if I can convince Mom to let me stay home today.

But before I can get up to ask her, Mom comes into my room and sits on my bed. "I have something to tell you," she says. I sit up.

"Anushri's mom called me late last night. Anushri's grandmother died yesterday."

"Oh, no! I know how much Anushri loved her grandmother!" I say.

"Anushri's mom left for India this morning," Mom says. "Anushri will be staying with us while her mother is gone. I know you will be a good friend to Anushri and help her through this very difficult time."

When I get to the bus stop, Anushri doesn't even look up at me. I don't know what to do, so I just say, "I'm really sorry to hear about your grandmother." She smiles a little bit, but I can tell she's trying not to cry.

All morning I try not to talk to anyone else or even look at anyone. I'm afraid that if I look at other kids, or talk to them, they'll say something about how strange I am. But no one says anything.

At recess, I meet Anushri by the monkey bars. I can see from her red eyes that she has been crying, but she seems a little bit better. "After school will you come over and help me pack?" she asks as she climbs on the monkey bars.

"Sure," I say. I'm glad there's at least one other person in my school who doesn't think I'm weird.

Directions: Read the questions and answers in column 1 on pages 16–19. Decide on the QAR for each question and write it in column 2. Decide on the appropriate evaluation for this answer and write the evaluation in column 3. Then, in column 4, write why you gave this evaluation.

QUESTION AND ANSWER	QAR

1. Why does the narrator's mother come into her room?
  A. to get her up because she is late for school
  B. to tell her breakfast is ready
  C. to tell her that her friend's grandmother died
  D. to tell her that she can't ride the bus to school
	1. _____

2. How does Anushri feel about her grandmother's death?
  A. she didn't really know her grandmother so she isn't sad
  B. she loved her grandmother so she is very sad
  C. she is angry because she can't go to India with her mother
  D. she is confused because she doesn't understand what is happening
	2. _____

3. Why did Anushri's mother go to India?
  A. she needs a vacation
  B. she misses her homeland
  C. she is moving back
  D. she is going to attend her mother's funeral
	3. _____

EVALUATION	HERE'S WHY
1. _____ _____ _____ _____	1. _____ _____ _____ _____
2. _____ _____ _____ _____	2. _____ _____ _____ _____
3. _____ _____ _____ _____	3. _____ _____ _____ _____

4. How does the narrator know that Anushri is feeling better?

   A. Anushri asks the narrator to help her pack

   B. Anushri's eyes are all red

   C. Anushri doesn't think the narrator is weird

   D. Anushri is silent at the bus stop

5. What could the narrator do to help Anushri feel better?

6. Who doesn't think the narrator is weird?

EVALUATION	HERE'S WHY
4. _____ _____ _____ _____ _____	4. _____ _____ _____ _____ _____
5. _____ _____ _____ _____ _____	5. _____ _____ _____ _____ _____
6. _____ _____ _____ _____ _____	6. _____ _____ _____ _____ _____

1. You are going to be in a book discussion group. Identify a book that many people in the class have read this year and then write two questions that will create opportunities for a good group discussion.

   Question: _____

   _____

   _____

   QAR: _____

   Question: _____

   _____

   _____

   QAR: _____

2. Imagine your class is preparing to learn about the history of your state. You are doing a KWL chart and have brainstormed a long list of things you already know about your state. Write two questions that could guide your class in a research project about the history of your state.

   Question: _____

   _____

   _____

   QAR: _____

   Question: _____

   _____

   _____

   QAR: _____

3. A new student has arrived in your class. She notices the charts and posters on the walls of the classroom. You point out several that you say are the most important. Identify those charts and posters and then write two questions that you could ask your new classmate to see whether she understands what the charts and posters say.

Charts and Posters: _____

Question: _____

_____

QAR: _____

Question: _____

_____

QAR: _____

4. If you were to help the teacher write questions to appear on an end-of-unit test, what subject would it be? Write two questions that the teacher could use on the test.

Subject: _____

Question: _____

_____

QAR: _____

Question: _____

_____

QAR: _____

Vultures

Lying on the forest floor a sick, old deer heaves its last breath. A few moments later a vulture circles above and swoops down. Soon more vultures arrive. The feast begins.

Although most biologists consider the vulture to be a kind of raptor, vultures are different from other raptors in many ways. Unlike hawks, falcons, eagles, and owls, vultures have small, weak talons and do not hunt for their food. Instead, they scavenge, searching far and wide for carrion. Vultures sometimes eat so much at once that they have trouble flying away after a big meal.

Some people think of vultures as garbage collectors. By eating dead animals, vultures help prevent the spread of disease and help keep the world clean.

Vultures also look a little different from other raptors. Instead of feathers, the heads of vultures are covered with skin. This is so that their faces can be easily cleaned after scavenging.

Vultures live on all the continents of the world except Australia and Antarctica. The Black Vulture is the most common North American vulture. They have black feathers and dark gray heads. Turkey Vultures also have black feathers, but their heads are colored bright red. Can you guess how they got their name?

Directions: Answer the questions below. Then write a question of your own. Identify the QAR for each.

1. How are vultures different from other raptors? _____

   _____

   _____

   _____

   QAR: _____

2. What is carrion? _____

   _____

   _____

   _____

   QAR: _____

3. How do you think the Turkey Vulture got its name? _____

   _____

   _____

   _____

   QAR: _____

4. Question: _____

   _____

   _____

   _____

   QAR: _____

Directions: Answer each question and read this text from *My Name Is Yun Jin* by Catherine Murphy. Then identify the QAR.

1. Do you have any ideas about what might happen next to Yun Jin?

_____

_____

_____

QAR: _____

The model was due in class that day, and Yun Jin kept glancing at it as he carried it to school. Every time he looked at his model, he felt as though he were back in Korea. He looked at it so often that he didn't see Ron Ellis until they bumped into each other and Yun Jin almost dropped his model.

"Hey, Stinker, watch where you're going!" cried Ron.

"My name is not Stinker. My name is Yun Jin," thought Yun Jin.

But Ron was so big and angry-looking that Yun Jin said nothing.

Before Yun Jin could walk away, Ron said, "What's this, a doll house?" He grabbed Yun Jin's model and pulled.

2. What did Yun Jin do as he carried his model to school?

_____

_____

_____

QAR: _____

3. What do you think Ron will do next?

_____

_____

_____

QAR: _____

"No!" cried Yun Jin, trying to hang on to his model, but Ron pulled so hard that the model's cardboard base ripped in two. All of the carts, tables, and cardboard people slid off, collapsing together in a heap in the wet, muddy gutter. Yun Jin stared in horror. The paint was smeared and the cardboard people were bent and broken. His project was ruined.

After Ron ran off, Yun Jin dropped the ruins of his project into a trash can and trudged into school empty-handed, his heart as heavy as a stone in his chest.

He didn't tell his teacher, Mrs. Ryan what had happened. How could he explain, when he spoke so little English? Instead, when Mrs. Ryan asked, "Where is your project, Yun Jin?" he just shook his head.

4. What happened to Yun Jin's project? _____

_____

_____

QAR: _____

5. What do you think Mrs. Ryan thought about Yun Jin's project?

_____

_____

_____

QAR: _____

Yun Jin usually gave his parents his tests and homework papers to look over, but he didn't show them the review sheet for his project. It had a sad face drawn under the grade of zero in Mrs. Ryan's green ink. If Apba knew what had happened, Yun Jin was sure he would never be proud of Yun Jin again.

6. Why didn't Yun Jin tell his parents about the project?

_____

_____

_____

QAR: _____

During the next few weeks at school, Ron teased Yun Jin every time he saw him. "Hey, Stinker!" he'd yell when he passed Yun Jin in the hallway. Each time, Yun Jin would think furiously, "My name is Yun Jin," but he didn't dare to say anything.

Ron came up behind Yun Jin on the playground and tugged on Yun Jin's backpack straps to make him fall over. He laughed at Yun Jin's clothes. He made fun of the food Yun Jin brought to school. He teased him about anything and everything. But each time, Yun Jin bit his lip and said nothing.

Questions:

_____

_____

_____

_____

_____

QAR: _____

_____

At school, Yun Jin avoided Ron as much as he could and looked forward to coming home at night. He looked forward even more to the weekends, when he helped his parents in the store and he didn't have to worry about going to school or seeing Ron Ellis for two whole days.

One Saturday morning, Yun Jin was placing juice cans on a shelf in the grocery store when the bell over the door jingled, and a customer walked in. When Yun Jin glanced up to see who it was, his heart turned cold. It was Ron Ellis.

Questions:

_____

_____

_____

_____

_____

QAR: _____

_____

Yun Jin felt like hiding behind a stack of boxes. "But that's what a little boy would do," he told himself. Instead, he kept placing cans on the shelf, as Apba had showed him.

Ron paid for a pack of gum. Then he turned and noticed Yun Jin.

"Hi, Stinker!" he said. Ron's smile might have fooled someone else into thinking that he and Yun Jin were friends, but Yun Jin knew better than to smile back. Silently, he watched Ron stroll out of the store.

"What did that boy call you?"

When Apba suddenly spoke from behind him, Yun Jin jumped. He hadn't known his father was there.

"He called me a stinker," mumbled Yun Jin uncomfortably.

Apba frowned. "What is that? An American nickname?"

Questions:

_____

_____

_____

_____

_____

_____

QAR: _____

Stunt People

A character in an adventure television show falls from the twentieth floor of an office building. The hero in an action-packed film is dragged underneath a truck, dives off a cliff, and gets blown up in an explosion—but lives to tell the tale. Whenever we watch a television show or a movie in which something dangerous happens to one of the characters, we are seeing a stunt person at work.

A stunt person performs a dangerous action, or stunt, in a film or television show. Some stunt people perform stunts, such as jumping a motorcycle over cars, during live shows.

Stunt people take precautions so that they will not be hurt when doing their stunts. Stunt people are trained so that they know how to safely perform stunts, such as falling and landing, and how to protect themselves by wearing padding and helmets. Stunt people also plan how to do their stunts down to the last little detail to reduce the risk of accidents.

Directions: Read each question carefully and select the best answer for the first three questions. For questions 4 and 5, write a brief, but complete, response.

1. Which of the following scenes would probably *not* require a stunt person?
   A. someone falls over a waterfall
   B. someone swims laps in a backyard pool
   C. someone jumps from a high building
   D. someone drives a car on winding roads at high speed

2. Where would you most likely see a stunt person?
   A. in a circus
   B. on a construction site
   C. at a racetrack
   D. in a film or TV show

3. Which of the following do stunt people usually wear?
   A. a fireproof suit
   B. an oxygen mask
   C. a safety rope
   D. none of the above

4. What kinds of training do stunt people have?

_____

_____

_____

_____

_____

_____

_____

_____

_____

5. Why do we need stunt people?

_____

_____

_____

_____

_____

_____

_____

_____

_____

_____

Snake Handlers

There are poisonous snakes in many countries throughout the world. Most of them are timid creatures who try to avoid people. However, if a poisonous snake is chased, stood on, or handled, it may bite. The venom of some snakes is mild and will only make a person sick. Others have a deadly venom that can kill.

Scientists use snake venom to make antivenin, which is an antidote for the poisonous venom. Antivenin is injected into the snakebite victim to fight the poison and to neutralize it, or make it harmless. A lot of snake venom is needed to make antivenin.

To make antivenin, snakes are kept in captivity and milked by specially trained snake handlers. The snake handlers face the danger of being bitten by deadly snakes. To avoid being bitten, a snake handler carefully picks the snake up, holding the snake tightly by the head so that it cannot bite.

The snake handler then places the snake's jaws around a rubber-capped bottle. The snake bites through the rubber cap and pumps its venom into the bottle. The snake handler then lets the snake go and sends the venom to a laboratory where the antivenin is produced.

Directions: After reading the text on page 30, brainstorm to plan what kinds of questions might appear on a standardized test. Then write at least two questions.

PLANNING IDEAS	QUESTIONS
_____	_____
_____	_____
_____	_____
_____	_____
_____	_____
_____	_____
_____	_____
_____	_____
_____	_____
_____	_____
_____	_____
_____	_____
_____	_____
_____	_____
_____	_____

The Peopling of America

People from other lands began to immigrate, move and settle, to the United States many years ago. Around 1820, immigration to the United States began to grow. It continued to grow during the rest of the nineteenth century. The numbers were highest around the turn of the century. However, during the years from 1930 to 1965, immigration to the United States slowed down a great deal.

One reason this happened was because of the Great Depression. This was a time when there was little money in the United States and jobs were hard to come by. Because of this, many immigrants had to return home to their native countries. When people in foreign lands saw all these people returning, they decided they did not want to go to America when they had little chance of making a good living.

Another reason immigration decreased in this time period was that World War II was happening in Europe. Many countries needed people to stay home and fight. When the U.S. entered the war, they became the enemy of some countries (Japan, Italy, and Germany). The U.S. would not let people immigrate from these countries. A final reason for fewer immigrants was that the U.S. had set restrictions during the 1920s. This limited the number of people that could enter the U.S. Some people in the U.S. felt that too many foreign people were allowed in.

When the war ended in 1945, U.S. president Harry S. Truman wanted to let immigrants back into the United States. He asked Congress to help him. They did. They passed the Displaced Persons Act of 1948. This act let hundreds of thousands of immigrants come to the U.S.

During this time period, more women than men entered the United States. Many of these women had American husbands whom they had met during the war in Europe. When the war ended, the soldiers came home. Later, they would send money so their wives could come to the U.S.

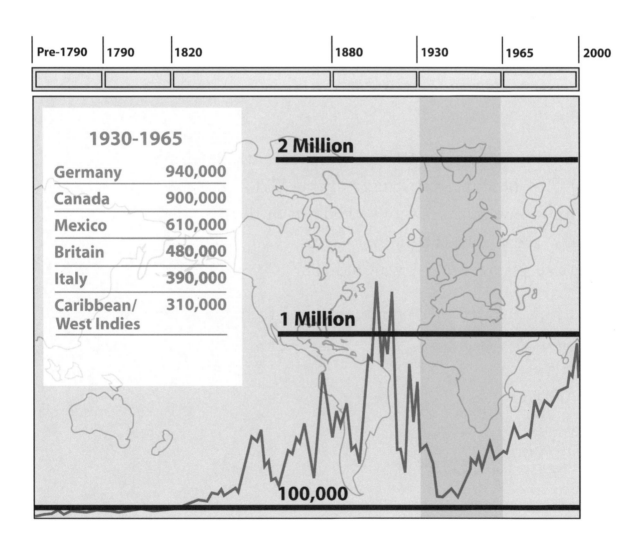

| Pre-1790 | 1790 | 1820 | 1880 | 1930 | 1965 | 2000 |

1930-1965

Germany	940,000
Canada	900,000
Mexico	610,000
Britain	480,000
Italy	390,000
Caribbean/ West Indies	310,000

2 Million

1 Million

100,000

QUESTION AND ANSWER

1. Which of the following is not a reason immigration to the United States decreased between 1930 and 1965?
   A. President Truman wouldn't let them in
   B. World War II was happening
   C. the Great Depression
   D. restrictions from the 1920s were still in place

2. Why did more women than men enter the U.S. between 1930 and 1965?
   A. they were finally able to travel alone
   B. they knew they could find good jobs in the U.S.
   C. they were coming to go to better colleges
   D. none of the above

3. Why do you think immigration increased after 1945?
   A. the U.S. lifted the restrictions of the 1920s
   B. more foreign people were kicked out of their homelands
   C. a new president brought new ideas
   D. the depression and the war ended

4. About how many total immigrants came to the U.S. between 1930 and 1965?
   A. 200,000
   B. 3,600,000
   C. 10,000,000
   D. 5,800,000

QAR	MY THOUGHTS
1. _____	1. _____
2. _____	2. _____
3. _____	3. _____
4. _____	4. _____

Directions: Read the text below from *Straight from the Horse's Mouth* by Judy Tertini. Then answer each question and identify the comprehension strategy that helped you answer the question.

Horses Through the Ages

The first horse that grazed on the earth was *eohippus*. Eohippus didn't look much like a horse— it was only the size of small dog, and instead of a hoof on each foot, eohippus had four toes on its fore feet and three toes on its hind feet. Gradually, new horses developed that were bigger and that had hoofs to help them run faster.

When people first appeared on the earth, they used horses for food. Then when people began to grow crops, they learned to tame horses, using them for carrying loads and pulling sleds. Soon, people were riding horses, too. Being on horseback gave a rider speed and power. Horses were a great advantage for hunting wild animals for food and fighting off enemies.

Over the years, horses have been used for transportation, as workhorses, and in wars. Today, however, horses are used mainly for enjoyment in sports and as pets.

QUESTION

1. How was eohippus different from today's horses?

2. How did people first use horses?

3. Why were horses an advantage for hunting and fighting?

4. Over the years, what have people used horses for?

ANSWER

1. _____

2. _____

3. _____

4. _____

STRATEGY

1. _____

2. _____

3. _____

4. _____

Ways Horses Move

Horses and ponies have four ways of moving. They can walk, trot, canter, and gallop.

The walk and gallop are the most natural movements for horses. Most breeds rarely trot in the wild, although some horses, such as the Hackney pony, have been bred for their trotting ability. Horses love to gallop and race each other, and this pace can be very exciting for an experienced rider.

At a walk, a horse moves each leg in turn. A rider should sit comfortably in the center of the saddle at this pace.

At a trot, diagonally opposite legs move together. A rider must learn to rise off the saddle and sit down again in time with the horse.

At a canter, the horse moves the two legs on each side together. A rider sits firmly in the saddle at this pace and leans forward and back with the rhythm of the horse.

At a gallop, the horse moves each leg quickly in turn. A rider should sit up out of the saddle and grip with the knees so as not to tire the horse.

Directions: Note the comprehension strategy listed. Read the text on page 38. Then write a question for each strategy so that someone answering the question must use that strategy to find the answer.

Scan:

_____

_____

_____

Find Main Idea:

_____

_____

_____

Summarize:

_____

_____

_____

Look for Important Information:

_____

_____

_____

Skim:

_____

_____

_____

_____

How the Buffalo Were Released on Earth

The people did not understand what this had to do with releasing the buffalo, but they knew that Coyote was a great schemer and they waited for him to explain. "I shall change myself into a killdeer," Coyote said. "In the morning when Humpback's son goes down to the spring to get water, he will find a killdeer with a broken wing. He will want this bird for a pet and will take it back into the house. Once I am in the house, I can fly into the corral, and the cries of a killdeer will frighten the buffalo into a stampede. They will come charging out through Humpback's house and be released upon the earth."

The people thought this was a good plan, and the next morning when Humpback's son came down the path to the spring, he found a killdeer with a crippled wing. As Coyote had foreseen, the boy picked up the bird and carried it into the house.

"Look here," the boy cried. "This is a very good bird!"

"It is good for nothing!" Humpback shouted. "All the birds and animals and people are rascals and schemers." Above his fierce nose Humpback wore a blue mask, and through its slits his eyes glittered. His basket headdress was shaped like a cloud and was painted black with a zigzag streak of yellow to represent lightning. Buffalo horns protruded from the sides.

"It is a very good bird," the boy repeated.

"Take it back where you found it!" roared Humpback, and his frightened son did as he was told.

Directions: Complete the chart by answering each question and then identifying the comprehension strategy that helped you to answer the question.

QUESTION AND ANSWER	STRATEGY
1. How did Coyote's plan work?	1.
2. What do you think Coyote will do next?	2.
3. What is a *rascal*? A *schemer*?	3.
4. What might be a good pet for Humpback's son?	4.

How the Buffalo Were Released on Earth

As soon as the killdeer was released it returned to where the people were camped and changed back to Coyote. "I have failed," he said, "but that makes no difference. I will try again in the morning."

The next morning when Humpback's son went to the spring, he found a small dog there. The boy picked up the dog at once and hurried back into the house. "Look here!" he cried. "What a nice pet I have."

"How foolish you are, boy!" Humpback growled. "A dog is good for nothing. I'll kill it with my club."

The boy held the dog and started to run away, crying.

"Oh, very well," Humpback said. "But first let me test that animal to make certain it is a dog." He took a coal of fire from the hearth and brought it closer and closer to the dog's eyes until it gave three rapid barks. "It is a real dog," Humpback declared. "You may keep it in the buffalo corral, but not in the house."

This of course was exactly what Coyote wanted. As soon as Humpback and his son went to sleep, Coyote opened the back door of the house. Then he ran among the buffalo, barking as loud as he could. When Coyote ran nipping at their heels, they stampeded toward Humpback's house and entered the rear door. The buffalo smashed down Humpback's front door and escaped.

Thus it was that the buffalo were released to scatter over all the earth.

Directions: Note each comprehension strategy listed. Read the text on page 42. Then write a question for each strategy so that someone answering the question must use that strategy to find the answer.

Scan:

_____

_____

_____

Find Main Idea:

_____

_____

_____

Summarize:

_____

_____

_____

Look for Important Information:

_____

_____

_____

Skim:

_____

_____

_____

_____

Peanut Butter and Jelly

As I was making peanut butter and jelly sandwiches for T.J. and Aidan the other day, I ran out of bread. I still had half a jar of peanut butter and close to three-fourths of a jar of jelly left.

As I ran down to the freezer to get another loaf of bread, I started thinking about the number of sandwiches I could make with the individual ingredients. A loaf of bread contains 18 slices, though the boys do not like to have heel sandwiches so we always feed those slices to the birds. The 16-ounce jars of peanut butter will make 12 sandwiches, and the 48-ounce jars of jelly will make 60 sandwiches.

If we were to start with a full loaf of bread and new jars of peanut butter and jelly, how many sandwiches could we make before emptying a bread bag and jars of jelly and peanut butter at the same time?

Solve the problem:

The Universe

There is the moon, there is the sun
Round which we circle every year,
And there are all the stars we see
On starry nights when skies are clear,
And all the countless stars that lie
Beyond the reach of human eye.

If every bud on every tree,
All birds and fireflies and bees
And all the flowers that bloom and die
Upon the earth were counted up,
The number of the stars would be
Greater, they say, than all of these.

by Mary Britton Miller

1. This poem is mostly about
   A. the moon
   B. the skies
   C. the stars
   D. fireflies

2. What do we circle "round" each year?
   A. the universe
   B. the moon
   C. the stars
   D. none of the above

3. When you read this poem, what do you picture in your mind?

   _____

4. How do you feel compared to the universe? _____

   _____

Anderson's Pumpkin Patch

Ms. Junco is the lead teacher for the fourth-grade team at Newton Elementary School. One week before Halloween, the team teachers assigned all of the fourth graders a new project. They thought that the students might enjoy making geometric jack-o'-lanterns, so they planned a field trip to Anderson's Pumpkin Patch to hunt, clean, and create the jack-o'-lanterns.

Looking at the class lists the night before the trip, Ms. Junco decided to put the students into groups so no one would have to work in the pumpkin patch alone. Her first attempt at using pairs did not work—one person was left out. Next she tried groups of five, but that didn't work either. Then she tried groups of three and again had someone left over. Still no luck when she tried groups of four. Each attempt ended with one person left out.

If each grade at Ms. Junco's school has fewer than 80 students, how many pupils are on her team?

Solve the problem:

QAR: _____

Travel

The railroad track is miles away,
    And the day is loud with voices speaking,
Yet there isn't a train goes by all day
    But I hear its whistles shrieking.

All night there isn't a train goes by,
    Though the night is still for sleep and dreaming
But I see its cinders red on the sky
    And hear its engine steaming.

 My heart is warm with the friends I make,
    And better friends I'll not be knowing,
Yet there isn't a train I wouldn't take,
    No matter where it's going.

by Edna St. Vincent Millay

1. What is this poem mostly about? _____

_____

_____

   QAR: _____

2. How does the poet feel about trains? _____

_____

_____

   QAR: _____

Energy and Tools

You can move an object by pushing it or pulling on it. The push or pull needed to make something move is called a force. When you make something move by using a force, you are doing work. Work means to apply a force to make an object move. However, the object must move some distance for your effort to be called work.

You need something else to do work. You need energy. Energy is the ability to do work or to cause changes in matter. Work cannot be done without energy. Energy is transferred from one thing to another.

A machine is anything that helps you do work or makes work easier. A simple machine is a machine with few parts. Many simple machines are called tools. There are six different types of simple machines. They are the lever, the pulley, the wheel and axle, the inclined plane, the screw, and the wedge. Ancient people may have been inspired by animals to invent tools.

A lever is a bar that can turn on a pivot or fixed point, called a fulcrum. Levers make it easier for people to lift heavy objects or open things. A lever doesn't make you stronger: it changes how much force you need to move something.

A pulley is made up of a rope, belt, or chain wrapped around a wheel with a groove in it. A wheel and axle are made up of a wheel and a bar that passes through the center of the wheel. An inclined plane is a flat, slanted surface. A screw is a spiral inclined plane. A wedge changes a downward or forward force into a sideways force.

Directions: Answer each question by circling the best answer for questions 1 and 2, and by writing a complete response for questions 3 and 4.

1. Work is

    A. when an object moves

    B. the energy it takes to move an object

    C. the act of applying a force to make an object move

    D. none of the above

2. Which of these is not a simple machine?

    A. a force

    B. a gear

    C. an inclined plane

    D. a lever

3. How are force, work, and energy related? _____

    _____

    _____

    _____

    _____

    _____

4. How might tools have been invented? _____

    _____

    _____

    _____

    _____

    _____

    _____

Animals Without Backbones

Invertebrates come in a variety of shapes and sizes. However, the one thing they have in common is that they lack a backbone. More than 95 out of every 100 animals are invertebrates. Invertebrates can be divided into smaller groups based on characteristics.

Sponges are the simplest invertebrates. A sponge's body is shaped like a sack with an opening at the top.

Cnidarians, such as jellyfish, are invertebrates that use poisonous stingers on tentacles to capture prey and for protection.

There are several kinds of worms. Flatworms have flat, ribbon-like bodies with a head and a tail. Roundworms have a slender, rounded body with pointed ends. The hookworm and vinegar eel are roundworms. Earthworms, sandworms, and leeches are segmented worms. They have more complex bodies than other worms.

Most seashells came from mollusks. Mollusks are soft-bodied. Some, like snails and slugs, live on land. Others, like clams and oysters, live in water.

Echinoderms are spiny-skinned animals. Echinoderms include starfish, sand dollars, sea cucumbers, and sea urchins. Echinoderms have an internal skeleton called an endoskeleton.

The largest group of invertebrates is made up of arthropods. An arthropod is an invertebrate with jointed legs and a body that is divided into sections. Arthropods have an exoskeleton, or a hard covering that protects an invertebrate's body. Included among arthropods are spiders, lobsters, centipedes, and insects.

Most of the animals on Earth are invertebrates. They are important because they are a food source for other animals. People also depend on them for many things.

Directions: Answer each question by circling the best answer for questions 1 through 3 and by writing a complete response for questions 4 and 5.

1. What is true about all invertebrates?
   A. they are a kind of sponge
   B. they have a common shape and size
   C. they make up 95% of all animals
   D. they do not have a backbone

2. Which is the largest group of invertebrates
   A. mollusks
   B. arthropods
   C. cnidarians
   D. echinoderms

3. Where do many of the invertebrates described here live?
   A. in water
   B. in the forest
   C. on other animals
   D. deep in the earth

4. Name two kinds of worms. Tell how they are alike and how they are different. _____

   _____

   _____

   _____

5. How might invertebrates be useful to people? _____

   _____

   _____

   _____

Directions: Answer each question as thoroughly as you can.

1. What is QAR? _____

_____

_____

_____

_____

2. How do you use QAR? _____

_____

_____

_____

_____

_____

_____

_____

_____

3. When do you use QAR? _____

_____

_____

_____

_____

_____

_____

Directions: Think about the knowledge you've gained about QAR this year. How have you changed the way you think about answering questions?

Directions: With your group, brainstorm a list of the various settings and situations that you can use QAR with during the rest of the school year.

Directions: Organize the information on page 54 so that it is more useful. You may use any kind of graphic organizer you would like, or an outline. Include enough detail and labels to ensure your organization will be clear to others.

QAR
Reflections
Journal